Goats On Your Lemonade Stand

Building Innovative Teams That Deliver

By Mike Duke

ISBN 978-0-9836830-0-1

Printed in the United States of America.

Dedication

This book is dedicated to my father, the Seer; my wife and best friend, a Shaper; and my children (Kyle, Nick, and Mackenzie) - Pilots, Builders, and Seers who inspire faith in a better future.

Introduction

Have you ever seen kids at a lemonade stand? They are absolutely glowing with enthusiasm. And you can bet the parents are off somewhere watching – rooting for their success! The parents might just be out there stopping traffic so their kids will get a chance to sell a cup or two.

During the construction of my daughter's lemonade stand, our extended family of pet goats made themselves at home (see book cover). Obviously, they did not know any better, but the promised cool refreshing glass of lemonade certainly lost a bit of its magic. This happens in our lives every day. Different innovative personalities come together to build a dream only to be thwarted by the Innovation Goats. The Innovation Goats come up with every reason why the dream will fail. They say stuff like **"We already tried that"**, **"that won't work"**, **"we don't do things that way"**. There is a way to turn those comments and the people that said them into a positive force for change.

I've been blessed to be part of teams that have created dozens and dozens of new inventions. It was not the tools and the processes they used alone that made the new innovations real. Their success resulted from the types of innovative personalities they represented and *how* they used the tools they chose.

Your lemonade stand might be a new invention, an innovative team, a company, or just an idea you've always wanted to make real.
We'll talk about how to align the right kind of innovative personalities with a process that delivers every time. Most importantly we'll figure out how to get the Goats off your lemonade stand.

Thank you for seeing things in a different way.

-- Mike Duke

Contents

Acknowledgements

I am indebted to so many for so much. Thank you to those listed and those also remembered in my heart.

- God: Thank you for your sacrifice, the countless blessings, and the chance to be something better than I deserve.

- Mom: Thank you for the immeasurable support and love.

- Kyle D.: Pilot, Seer and Builder, I can't wait to see what you come up with!

- Nick D.: Seer and Pilot, the world seeks your calm and vision.

- Mackenzie and Karen D.: Seers, you both see the world in more colors than most of us know. Thank you for your artful vision!

- Dmitri M.: Thanks for being a good friend and Builder.

- Glen G.: The best mentor ever and the most powerful Seer / Pilot combo!

- Jeff Deluca: Thank you for Feature Driven Development!

- Kourtney E.: Most excellent Copy Editor.

1

PEOPLE, PROCESS, AND PROTOTYPES

"People are very open-minded about new things—as long as they're exactly like the old ones."
Charles F. Kettering (Pilot!)

People, Process, and Prototypes represent the combination that creates value. One would think that such a simple formula would be easy to implement. But, for some reason, we tend to get these elements of innovation delivery mixed up. Each component has its own complexities, but none more important than the people part. We'll discuss how to identify, align, and set into motion the right kinds of innovation personalities. Sometimes process and prototypes get all the attention when all along they should be created to support the people. Not the other way around.

Once we've got the right people, we'll focus on the Process. Surprisingly simple to understand, it can be very difficult to sustain. Finally, execution is nothing without a Prototype. Again, I want to emphasize that we are creating a process and a prototype engine that will serve the personalities driving the vision.

Speaking of interesting personalities my best friend's dad down the street, Mr. Smelcer, used to make the best biscuits. On Sunday afternoons, you would usually find him up to his elbows in flour with a Marlboro perched just below his long mustache. If you could get past the 2 inch ash ledge, you would be amazed to see that the biscuits he was baking were about a pound each and larger than two fists. You could add honey and butter, jelly, or just dip them in your brown gravy, but they were good plain, right out of the oven. Even though he was the best biscuit baker in Georgia, I would never ask him to bake me a cake. He couldn't match 3 colors together. He constructed his biscuit product with a recipe and process that was drilled into his head since he was splitting wood in the hills of Tennessee as a boy.

I tried to replicate his recipe years later (working at a local fried chicken restaurant), but could never pull it off. It seems we need more than just the ingredients to make magic. And it wasn't just his oven that made the biscuits – so there is more to it than the tools.

Technique and experience are required to make the perfect buttery biscuit. Those are human characteristics. Not just a recipe or tool. We'll go through the people process that bridges innovation and application. We'll talk briefly about the prototyping process as well (the bread and butter of the innovation world) because our personalities of innovation delivery thrive on incremental success! But first, let's talk about the flour in the innovation biscuit: People (Seers, Shapers, Pilots, Builders, and the ever present – Goat.)

GOATS ON YOUR LEMONADE STAND

2

THE PERSONALITIES OF INNOVATION DELIVERY

"The meeting of two personalities is like the contact of two chemical substances; if there is any reaction, both are transformed."
Carl Gustav Jung (Shaper!)

About four years previous to the writing of this book, I was fortunate enough to witness a people mixing miracle. My boss at the time asked me to "ideate" (come up with some new stuff) around a particular topic. As I had no idea how to do this, I decided to invite a few of my friends to the session. I carefully selected friends who I knew would make me look good. So I grabbed six names out of the hat and invited these very different personalities to the meeting.

By the end of this particular session, we had gathered over 71 features for a new product that would go on to be patented. I was astonished. Today, there are variations of the product that this team dreamed up all over the world, but we had it pegged years ago. So I was left to ponder - what in the world just happened? At this meeting, there were a couple technical folks, two or three business people (one very passionate about everything), and at least one nut case. Oh and there was also that infamous "defensive player" (the Goat) who was sure it would never work. Somehow that mixture of personalities had come together (some meeting for the first time) to create a powerful new product that nobody had ever considered. What was the magical formula? After dozens of these kinds of sessions, a personality trend evolved for those teams that were extremely productive.

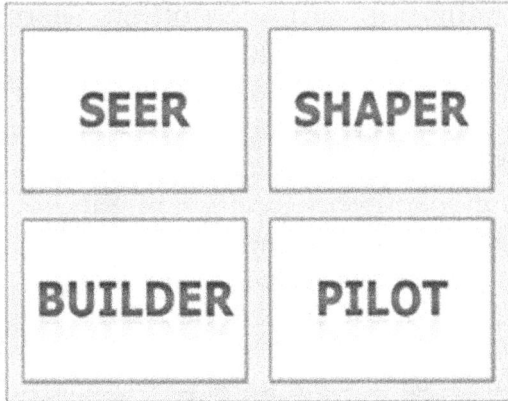

Figure 1. The Personalities of Innovation Delivery

Note that the caption for Figure 1 does not simply say the "Personalities of Innovation." There are millions of those. These are the personalities of Innovation *delivery*. We will discuss these personalities, how to interact with them, and how they interact together to deliver a product, service, or prototype.

Delivery in this context means that we start with some raw ingredients (a vision or two) and end up with something you can touch, something real, and something valuable.

One of the first challenges you face with getting innovation delivery off the ground is to identify which people around you fall into each type.

Important note: These personality types don't hang out with each other. Seers are not fond of Shapers. Builders have little patience for Pilots. Shapers like Pilots and can't stand Seers. So you can probably imagine that if you need one of each of these types (at a minimum) working together why this might not happen naturally. We'll talk more about these behavior patterns and how to coax them into a cohesive unit in the next chapter.

If you can manage to get at least one of each of these personality types in your corner, you are on the way to creating new value from innovation. All too often however there are goats that get in the way. Like my father always says – "Nothing smells worse than a wet goat."

THE PERSONALITIES

GOATS ON YOUR LEMONADE STAND

3

THE SEER

SEER	SHAPER
BUILDER	PILOT

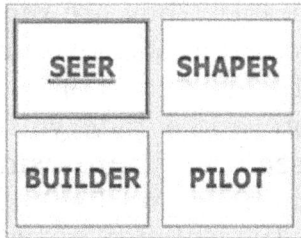

"Cherish your visions and your dreams as they are the children of your soul; the blueprints of your ultimate achievements."
Napoleon Hill (Seer!)

The Seer is the easy one to spot. Usually this person is easy to find because they're the loudest ones in the room and they usually get all the credit. You might also know them as the "Big Idea" people! They use phrases like:

"Why can't we just...."
"This should be so much simpler...."
"What were they thinking?"
"We can change the world by just...."
"I've got it! Let's just...."

It's important to list these clues. OK, the Seers aren't always loud, but they do always use these words. While Seers can be annoying, they are invaluable. They are the passion I refer to throughout this book. You need them. So deal with it. If you are one of them, God bless you. I love you, and I hate you. Those of us who cannot "see" the future using your gift of imagination simply stand back in awe. My father is a Seer. I've watched my whole life as he has automated the world around him.

Real Seers are actually the rarest of the four personalities, but they do get most of the press and for that reason, they seem to be everywhere. Seers say things like:

"Why can't we just find a way to disable text messaging in a moving automobile? Maybe there should be some kind of text suppression device in the steering wheel or tires?"

Want to get a Seer on your team?

The *right* questions to ask a Seer include:
- "We've failed at this before, how can we...."
- "What's your prediction for this market, tool, and problem?"
- "Have you been feeling pain with this lately? There has to be a better way...."

Notice we used some of their phrases above: "There has to be a better way." The fact of the matter is there is no better way to set a Seer on fire. Try it...watch what happens—and be prepared to take notes.

The *wrong* questions to ask a Seer include:
- "How can we 'chunk this up?'" This means de-scope or take bits away from.
- "What's the value proposition here?" A Seer might just take a swing at you.
- "Has this been done before?"

What does success look like for the Seer? I realized this answer while helping my Grandmother-in-law install a bird feeder in her backyard. When her granddaughter, grandson-in-law, and great grandchildren were all together with her, installing that feeder in her backyard, there were tears in her eyes after we finished. It wasn't the stupid bird feeder. It was having the support for her that made that day and that project special. When Shapers, Builders, and the Pilot gather to turn a Seer's vision into something special, it creates a magical moment. I've seen it time and time again as my team has created a working proto-type for someone. At the time the prototype is unveiled, the Seer doesn't care about money, pride, or whose idea it was. They just know that people believed in their vision and made it real. That is all the incentive that the Seer will ever need.

Unfortunately, your Seers will be under constant attack by the Goats. The Goat targets the loudest voice. They fire "zingers" in meet-ings that have no logical response. Seers are usually ill-equipped to deal with the Goat and will shut down – killing the energy in the room.

The Seer is a powerful force on any innova-tion delivery team, but they are one of the most easily disheartened. In my experience, Seers are who they are because it's ingrained in their DNA. That means they have been at-tacked since they started telling people that they just saw things a little differently. Keep that in mind and pay special attention to how to manage your goats later in the book. Edu-cate your Seers on how to respond. Respond for them if you have to. Protect your Seer – they are the energy source for innovation de-livery.

Raw energy is not enough though. Everyone can feed off the energy of a good idea, but if nothing ever becomes real – it's just as much of a downer. Bring the Shaper!

GOATS ON YOUR LEMONADE STAND

4

THE SHAPER

SEER	**SHAPER**
BUILDER	PILOT

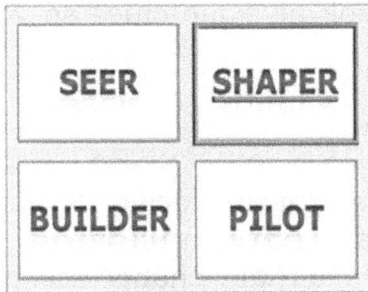

"Planning is bringing the future into the present so that you can do something about it now"
Alan Lakein (Shaper!)

The Shaper is the rarest amongst us. If you find a Shaper, embrace them. Really, reach out and hold them tight. Do not let them leave...ever. Why? You need the Shaper for the productization process (this is where cash flow is born). The Shaper usually has no creative ability in a vacuum (I know there are always exceptions), but if you put them in a room with a Seer or two, you could end up with five new products and 100 new features each. OK, if they are so great, why don't we ever hear about them? They are usually not the loudest voice in the room. As a matter of fact, they usually won't speak unless you draw them out. Let's look at some clues so you can find them first:

Shapers use phrases like:
"What if you just...."
"I just don't get this idea..." (Goatish I know)
"That idea is crazy, but if you..."
"You could actually change this part and..."

When prompted with an idea:
Idea: "The power company just should have sent me a text message telling me that my bill was overdue. They should just zap me through my phone to let me know when to send a payment."

Shaper responses:
"They should send a text before you're due."

"They should allow you to respond to the text."

"They should have known this was a bad bill month for you and extended payments with your permission."

In case you missed it, the Shaper is breaking the Seer's ideas in to parts over time. They are harvesting value through a process called "featurization." Examples from above include:
Feature 1: "Pre-Warn Text Me."
Feature 2: "Interactive Power Texting."
Feature 3: "Know-Me Billing."

The Feature Function development process (borrowed "Feature Driven Design" from one of my Shaper heroes, Jeff Deluca) comes naturally to the Shaper.

If you manage to get a Seer and a Shaper in the same room – congratulations! That is not easy. Again, these people don't hang out with each other. Having these two personalities together is an almost unnatural act. Seers think their concept is perfect and needs very little work. The shaper couldn't care less, but is usually annoyed with the Seer's lack of "reality." So there is work to do here to get them creating cash.
Want to get a Shaper on your team?

Here are questions for your Shaper:
"What do you think of Mary's idea?"

"What can we add to bring this back to reality?"

"When do you think this feature or that feature might make sense to take to market?"

Notice that we gradually moved from the word "idea" or concept to a discussion of "features." This is because shapers don't speak in terms of "horizontal product offerings." In other words, they don't talk about big picture perspectives. Instead, they focus on incremental delivery and value added. Version 1.0 is what they need to pay for the adventure – and that's all your Shaper can think of.

Your Seer will be happy that we're talking about implementation and ignore the fact that we just whittled their idea down to 2 or 3 primary features. It's not deception—it's inception. If you are the Seer here, remember that nobody shoves a new flavor in their mouth without a small taste. And if it's good enough, people will pour cash into the final product.

Success for the Shaper

This varies a bit, but in my experience, the Shaper needs checkpoints. If those checkpoints are reached, success has been reached. Incremental progress is important to the Shaper. Three and four year projects with no incremental successes will lead to Shaper turnover, politics, and unnecessary drama. I wish it were more exciting than that, but it's not. Shapers like delivery, but incremental delivery is enough. One of my favorite Shaper comments of all time – "We hit 72 out of 103 milestones but the project went belly up. That means we beat the odds and won this one." Notice – the project went belly up and the team was dissolved, but the Shaper walked away with a "live to fight another day" attitude. If you are a Seer – you're thinking "All that work and nothing to show for it." If you are a shaper, you are thinking – "wow, 103 milestones – big project – sounds like fun."

Now, we've got the big idea person and someone who is shaping that concept into something real. Now we need someone who can make it real enough to take it to the next level. We need a Builder.

GOATS ON YOUR LEMONADE STAND

5

THE BUILDER

SEER	SHAPER
BUILDER	PILOT

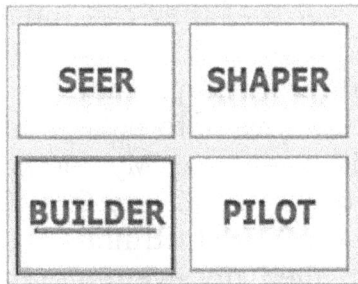

"A spirit with a vision is a dream with a mission..."
Song lyrics - "Mission" by Neil Peart

The Builder is not just the roofer, the coder, the painter, or the person with a practical skill set. A Builder is someone who can hear a vision and take ownership of it. Most people get excited about their own ideas. Builders get excited about others' ideas. When a Seer adequately shares their vision, a Builder will make it real. Builders are also very good at pulling together bits of existing resources (they are leverage experts) to make a solution real. So why can't a builder just build their own ideas? The Builder's ideas usually suck. Crude, I know. Builders are happiest assembling tools and other tangible assets to create something real that they can touch. They don't really spend a lot of time solving problems with imagination (ironically, they do tend to like video games). I went to college (the first time) to write video games. My focus was on the power languages like C and C++. Complex data structures and algorithmic logic were the things that filled my evenings and weekends. The video game revolution was just getting going, and I was going to create the next big video game. Look out Ms. Pac-Man, here I come!

I sat down one day to write that first game, and after several hours of moving dots around on the screen, I knew I was in trouble. Yup, I was a Builder. I couldn't match two colors together—much less come up with an intriguing game that would keep people's interest. I thought to myself, "Crap, now what?"

Builders are generally depressed about this reality. There are some Builders out there who are also Seers. But it is very rare when all these innovative personalities are built into one person. Maybe you know one? I've personally never met one. Though there was this TV show in the '80s about a guy with a mullet who could solve any problem (more about that later). But he's the only one I've ever seen.

Success for the Builder

I remember coding for days on my Commodore 64. Day and night, I slaved over an amazing application. When I finished it, I ran out of the room to find my mother. "Mom, I finished the app!" She followed me back to my room. I pushed the magic button and...ta-da! The words "Hello Mom!" bounced from one end of the screen to the other. As you might imagine, her response was less than enthusiastic.

Builders get satisfaction from being a part of the creation process. There must be something tangible created that they can look back on. The longer it lasts – the better. One example: Programmers insert secret chunks of code in mainstream software applications. With the right combination of keys, the "Easter Egg" would pop-up. One of my favorites from a major computer software company would clear the screen and fill it with floating jelly donuts. If you clicked on one of the donuts, a pro-grammer's face might appear. This was proof that the Builder had a part in the building—even if it was only one block of concrete in the skyscraper. "Legacy" is important to the Builder. By the way, if you clicked the wrong jelly donut – a picture of Elvis would pop out instead.

THE BUILDER

GOATS ON YOUR LEMONADE STAND

6

THE PILOT

SEER	**SHAPER**
BUILDER	**PILOT**

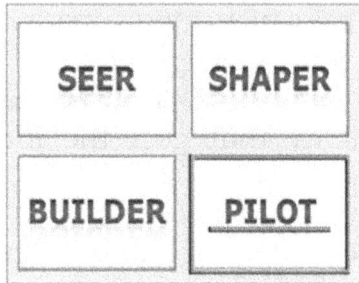

"We must become the change we want to see."
Mahatma Gandhi (Pilot, Seer & Shaper)

Some might confuse the Pilot with a leader or project manager. That would be incorrect. A leader or project manager sails a boat through sometimes rough waters because they have to. They keep the project moving in the right direction on the most direct path. The Pilot sails into the storm on purpose at full speed, because they know that is where they'll find things that no one else will ever see. The Pilot is courageous but courteous, kind but direct, and most important, the Pilot, through the faith of the team, never loses sight of the impossible path. The pilot believes in the innovation team. Without that faith, even a strong leader will hesitate. Pilots do not hesitate. That is why they get their teams to the finish line every time. This is why the Pilot is the personality that gets the innovation into the delivery phase.

Pilots are leaders of foundations, community service groups, neighborhood watch teams, or even the winning coach of your child's sports team. Pilots are leaders of companies and leaders of small teams. The only thing that separates them from other leaders is faith and courage. They took chances: Some paid off; some did not. But in every case, their success was delivered through pure will and determination backed through teams of Seers, Shapers, and Builders. Their teams executed on vision. And if you can do that, you can name your job, your future, and your title as a Pilot.

Success for the Pilot

One hundred projects later, the Pilot will refer back to the successful products as the ones that made the biggest difference in people's lives: The lives of her team and those that consumed the product created. Even if a product was never created, the friendships and teamwork created under the faith and leadership of the Pilot represent success.

GOATS ON YOUR LEMONADE STAND

7

THE GOAT

"No pessimist ever discovered the secret of the stars or sailed to an uncharted land or opened a new heaven to the human spirit."
Helen Keller

You have seen this personality in every team you have ever worked with. This is the anti-innovation personality. You'll recognize them at home, at work, at any volunteer job, or even on your favorite reality television show.

Common goat comments (and what should be your response):
1. "That won't work." When asked why, they respond, "Just because."
   a. Your response: "Draw me a picture of the worst case scenario you can envision."
2. "I don't get it and never will."
   a. Your response: "Not all ideas are for everyone, but I appreciate your honesty."
3. "It's just a...." Fill in the blank with a generic comment about your idea. I hate this comment the most.
   a. Your response: "It means a lot to me, our customer, our team, our friends, our [fill in the blank]. What can we do together to make it more important?"
4. "We already did that, and it did not work."
   a. Your response: "Maybe the idea's time has come. We'll work together so the vision gets a second chance."
   b. Another response: "If we try again and it makes a difference, we both win this time."
   c. Yet another response: "Great! We can learn from your experience and make it happen together!"

These responses will help you place the Goat's opinions in the right category. What ever happens, don't forget that your Pilot, Seers, Shapers, and Builders outnumber the Goats. Teams without Goats move quickly to create new products. But innovations that last for generations always have a Goat or two on their team. They use the Goat personalities to challenge their team. I believe that with nothing to push against we rarely grow. Also, convert your Goat to a Shaper and its guaranteed money. I've only seen one Pilot pull this transformation off – that Pilot's team patented their idea.

Success for the Goat

A real Goat will only feel successful when their perceived risks have been mitigated and more importantly they feel like their position is clearly understood. Even if the team pushes a product into production and is declared a success, the Goat will argue otherwise.

If you convert the Goat to a Shaper, success will then mean something different. How do you convert a Goat into a Shaper? Only a strong Pilot can pull this off. Why? The Pilot has faith in her team. She will have to understand and own her team's vision. That understanding is the foundation for the conversion.

GOATS ON YOUR LEMONADE STAND

8

MIXING THE
PERSONALITIES

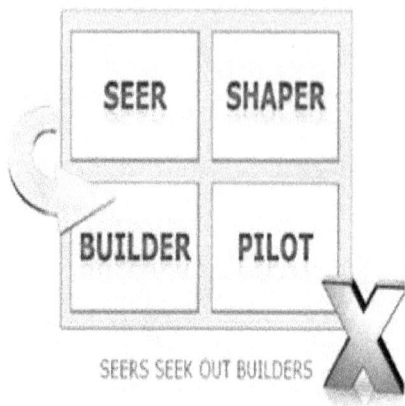

Figure 2. Seers Seek Out Builders

So what happens when these personalities come together? What happens when you mix the ingredients in the wrong order? It may look like a biscuit, but it will taste like a boot strap.

Seers instinctively seek out builders (Figure 2.) Why? Because they are aching to see their visions become real. This is the most common combination I've seen.

Instant gratification for the Seer—they get something built. The problem is that nobody usually wants it. See below.

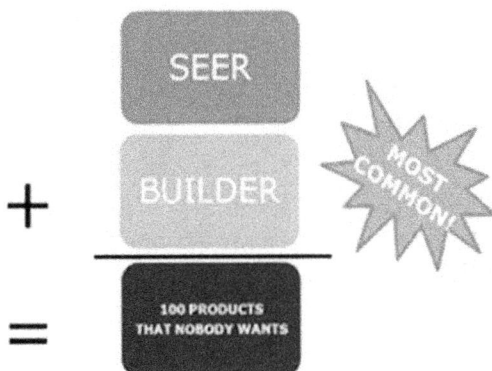

Figure 3. Seers + Builders = Crap

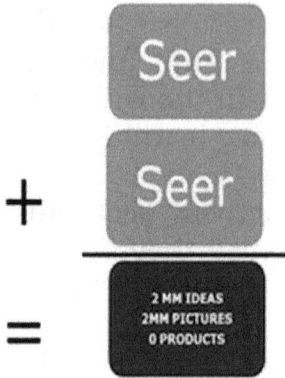

Figure 4. Seers + Seers = 0 Products

So what happens when Seers get together?
A. Arguing.
B. Pictures.
C. More Pictures.

Visionaries have a lot in common so they do tend to flock together, but they usually lack the ability to break a vision down into working parts. Leveraging stuff lying around to build a prototype is usually a little out of the realm of possibility as well. So we're left with ideas and hand drawn pictures. Cool, but no cash.

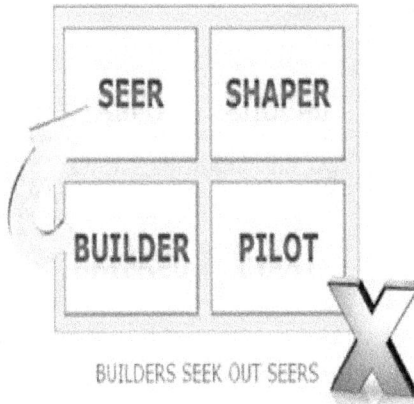

Figure 5. Builders Seek Out Seers

As Builders, we are drawn to those who have vision. Those people who can bring imaginative solutions to every day problems. Builders are also looking for what we call the "money people." Unfortunately, even though the Builders might make some money from the Seer, the product is still crap and that need—to make a difference—is not realized.

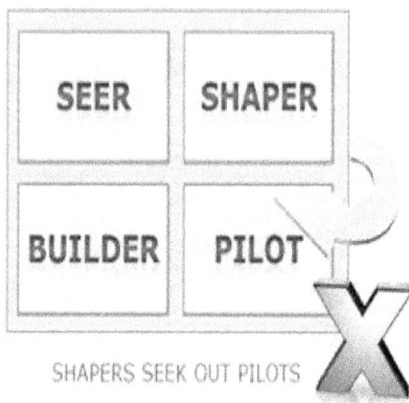

Figure 6. Shapers Seek Out Pilots

What about the Shapers? Those people who can break a fantasy down into logical parts that generate revenue? Who are they usually spotted with? In my experience, Shapers hang out with other Shapers, but occasionally, you'll find them with the Pilots. So why do Shapers seek out Pilots? Pilots are the courageous and bold leaders. Shapers look for that continuity and security.

This sounds like a joke, but it's not. What do you get when you get a bunch of Shapers together?

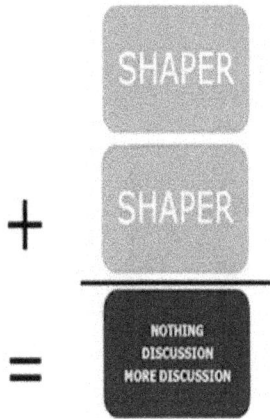

Figure 7. Shapers + Shapers = Documentation

Not much happens when you bring Shapers together. You might get:

    A. Documentation (and usually guilt from analysis paralysis).

    B. Reuse of existing product ideas.

    C. More documentation.

These powerful personalities are classically known for analysis paralysis. If you've ever been on one of these teams where nothing ever seems to be created—other than documentation, meetings, and more documentation—you've been in Shaper Hell. For as powerful as a Shaper is in the right environment, they can be completely useless in a vacuum. They can be even more useless when accompanied by only the Pilot.

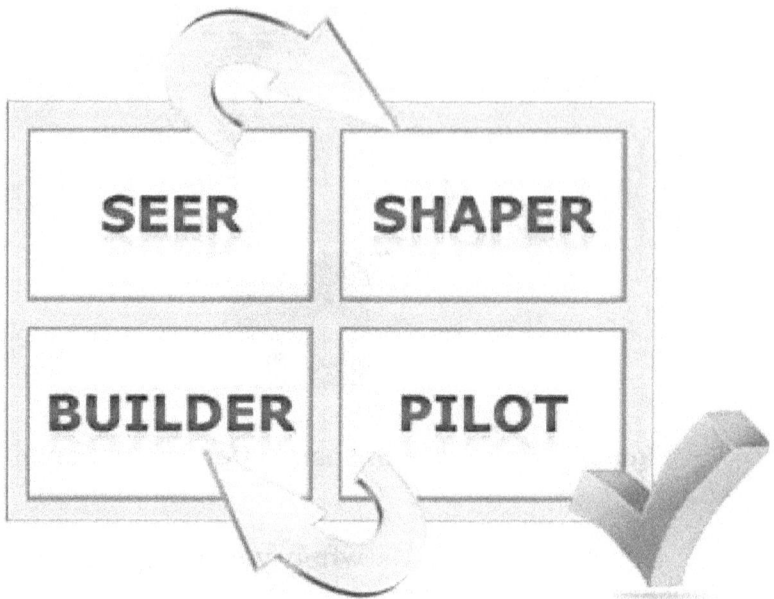

Figure 8. The Successful Combination

When the right idea is introduced to the right people for the right reason at the right time, innovation delivery is guaranteed.

Seers provide the vision. Shapers break that vision down into parts that fit on a realistic timeline. Builders construct prototypes that empower the team to see the vision together and Pilots keep them all in motion.

Summary

So these four personalities are everywhere, and I know what you're thinking - they are not always exclusive. There are Seers who have Builder in them. There are Builders who have Shaper in them. But is there anyone out there that has Pilot, Seer, Shaper, and Builder personality traits? YES! His name is MacGyver! Remember that TV show? (Google it, kids). One person, who could in a flash, see the problem, shape the solution, use bits of things around him to solve the problem—and then usually blow something up. We were mesmerized by this character because it was something unreal and we wanted to be like him. In all seriousness, there are personalities out there like this, but they are the rarest of rare and I've never met one...yet.

All this can seem a bit overwhelming, but by now you may have recognized some attributes of these personalities in yourself. Let's examine this from your point of view.

GOATS ON YOUR LEMONADE STAND

9

YOUR INNOVATIVE
PERSONALITY

"Know that you yourself are a miracle."
Norman Vincent Peale

YOU ARE THE SEER

You have an amazing idea, but have no idea how to get it to market. Now what?

1. Be prepared to share the idea. But what about protection? Print out a NDA (Non Disclosure Agreement) from the Internet, and make people sign it if you want to feel better. But it's pretty much a waste of time: Unless you've hooked up with a Shaper or Builder, your idea is just an idea and not very marketable.

2. You need features. Anything anyone will ever care to buy has to be broken into features. Find a Shaper. How? Use questions listed in chapter 3. You don't have to talk specifically about your idea to find your Shaper. When you do find them, hang on to them. Buy them lunch, coffee, or both if you have to. And for mercy's sake, bring something to write with.

3. You and your Shaper now need a Builder. No, I don't mean a SME (Subject Matter Expert). You need someone who can hear your idea and the features, take ownership of the concept, and begin to build the working model or prototype.

4. Finally, you can play the Pilot because you have the vision—or find the craziest A-type personality you can to help bring the solution

home.

YOU ARE THE SHAPER

You are the key to any real innovation delivery. Don't forget to write yourself into the business plan when a Seer or Pilot shows up looking for your gift. Be patient with the Seer. Their imaginations remain on fire—even when the dream is realized. You and the Builder are kindred spirits: The more you know, the greater the unknown. If you choose to bring your creative perspective to this partnership, you will adopt a vision as one adopts a child: You will help nurture an idea through maturity and talk about it for years to come as it moves into its own.

If you didn't get that last paragraph, you are not a Shaper.

YOU ARE THE BUILDER

Find a concept to love, and make it last as long as possible. You, above all, will pay the price for the Seer's vision—for better or worse. Sweat, dedication, and love for a vision made real will keep you energized. The money that will be derived from the concept's creation won't hurt either.

1. Seers will find you. Don't follow the Seer

alone. Find the Shaper to help bring the vision to realistic implementation.

2. Shapers will bore you. Sorry Shapers, breaking a vision down into profitable parts is boring to a builder.

3. Never try to build a production product without a mixture of the two personalities (Seer and Shaper). If you try to build from the Seer alone, you will waste countless hours on promises made by him. Don't even trust the market research they bring to you. It doesn't matter.

4. Never try to build a production product from a Shaper who doesn't "own" the vision. If they have no passion for the idea, you will have no payment for it.

YOU ARE THE PILOT

When you hear a vision that just makes sense, you know how to bring the parts together to create the whole. You are a mirror of the Seer's energy. Share that energy with the other innovation personalities on your team as often as possible. They will lean on you – not the inventor. Seek out the personality types that you can have undeniable faith in and get busy getting things out of their way. Mitigate the fear expressed by the Shaper. Exaggerate the inventor's sanity, and most importantly – encourage your builders to own the vision.

YOU ARE THE GOAT

Through your persistent fear of the un-known, an innovation team will mitigate their risk. With your consistent history lessons, an innovation team will be able to see the future. And finally as a member of an innovative team, you will find yourself where you never thought you would – you are one of the crazy people who came together to change things.

YOU DON'T KNOW WHO YOU ARE

You are not alone. After speaking at several events, the most common question I get is "So what am I?" Since I just met most people that ask that question – I really have no idea. But there are a series of questions I've learned to ask that might help. You will find a short sur-vey that will steer you in the right direction at AreYouAGoat.com.

IS YOUR TEAM INNOVATIVE?

If you are the leader of a company, team, or even a small volunteer group, this is a fun way to strike up a conversation. Send the web site link along to those you are curious about. If you are wondering why your group seems to be less than innovative, you may have a group full of shapers. If your team never seems to be able to come up with something new – you might be missing the Seer.

CAN YOU DO THIS BY YOURSELF?

In my opinion, we were not meant to create things alone. Even if you could create something brand new by yourself, you might find that the joy in doing so will be short lived. When people are successful with innovation delivery, they rarely talk about the product as much as they talk about the people they interacted with along the way to make it real.

YOU'RE READY

OK, now you have the right mixture of personalities (even a Goat or two). It's time to build the future. In the next chapter, we'll cover how to direct these resources to create value. It involves one last leap of faith. Actually, no leap needed. We're going to build a bridge.

YOUR INNOVATIVE PERSONALITY

GOATS ON YOUR LEMONADE STAND

10

THE INNOVATION
BRIDGE PROCESS

"What need the bridge much broader than the flood?"

William Shakespeare (SEER)

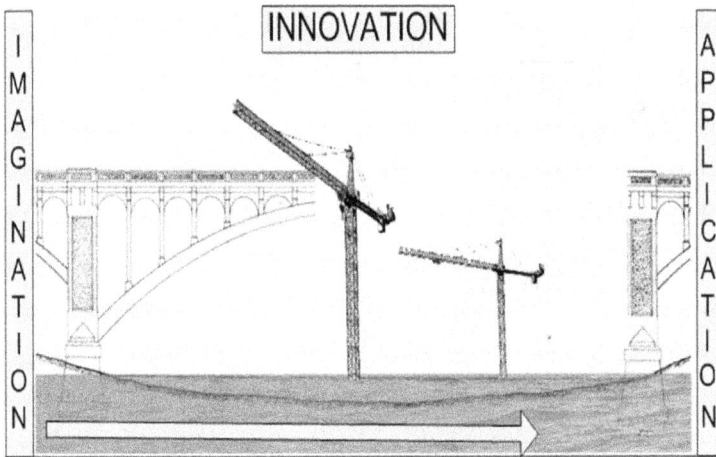

Figure 9. Bridging Imagination & Application

Imagination, innovation, and application are three power words that define growth. You've heard about those legends that just had a simple idea that made millions. The solution in hindsight usually leaves us saying to ourselves, "Why didn't I think of that?" Well, we are going to tell you why you didn't think of it and why you never will. Or would, depending on whether or not you read Section 2. First, the big picture—actually, only about five inches wide. I scratched this picture together forever ago and just can't let it go. Please pardon the rough look.

Figure out how to cross this bridge and you won't need any rainbows to get your pot of gold. We'll show you how to get this bridge built and make it sustainable. Most people have the materials for the bridge delivered to the job site and never actually build the bridge. Think about it...how many times do you hear, "We collected thousands of ideas" or that the innovation was an "accident" (i.e. not repeatable).

Imagination

The author of this book can honestly say that he's never had a unique thought in his life. Fortunately, it's not required. You may have just taken a sigh of relief. Creativity is a difficult (if not impossible) thing to learn (a failed art class in primary school might come to mind). There are a lot of people out there who simply have little to no imagination. No worries—they usually manage to score big on the other two elements: innovation or application.

Innovation

Now let's quickly talk about the difference between imagination and innovation. (And let's ward off the letters first by saying that this is the author's perception of these two terms. There are probably hundreds of others.) For the sake of argument, let's say that imagination is pure thought that has very little to do with any elements of reality. In other words, what can be imagined has no ties to what we might consider to be part of our world. Innovation, however, can best be summed up in this example. A Russian friend of mine, Dmitry, and I used to play chess every day at lunch at our favorite Mexican restaurant. One day while pondering yet again how he would destroy me with his Queen's knight, I spilled some red salsa on my white shirt. I knew that salsa stain would speak for me for the rest of the day—meetings, hallway conversations, etc. No matter what I said, everyone's eyes would be drawn to the large ugly red stain. Dmitry, sensing my dismay, suggested defending myself with my King's bishop and also removing the stain ASAP. He went on by saying that if I used the table salt, napkin, and a bit of water it would lift the stain almost immediately. It worked! By using assets immediately available (leverage), I was able eliminate the stain (add value) just in time to lose the game...again. That was innovation in its finest hour. Using stuff you already have to create new value.

Application

In this context, application refers to doing something, anything, which is applied. This can be a document, prototype, clay ball, spit wad, you name it. If you create something modeled after an idea, you have "application." So what? This is a really big deal! Unfortunately, it's where most innovation hits the wall. Not because people are lousy at it, but because painters stink at plumbing. That will make more sense later.

Build the Bridge

My favorite cartoon as a child (and as an adult—who am I kidding?) was a cat and a canary. The cat was fed up with the bird, so he loaded an old musket that he took down off the wall with the intention of removing the annoying canary. He couldn't remember exactly which went first: the bullet or the powder. So he added the powder and dropped the bullet in. He then began to pack it when the gun went off shooting him into the ceiling. He crawled through the upper floor, came down the stairs, and this time, put the bullet in first, then the powder. He began to pack it in, and once again, the gun went off. On his third attempt, the camera panned down to the canary that kept pulling the trigger. We might have all the right personalities and the right idea, but if we don't pull the trigger at the right time, you're just left with an idea (and powder burns).

What happens if we have all the right innovative personalities, but fail to execute in the right order? When we mix innovation personalities the wrong way, the gun goes off in our faces with projects in the red, going over budget, or just never getting started. When we get the personalities right, but execute poorly, we are left with more and more ideas that go no where. We need a safe bridge to get our concept from imagination through to application.

The Bridge Process – 16 Weeks

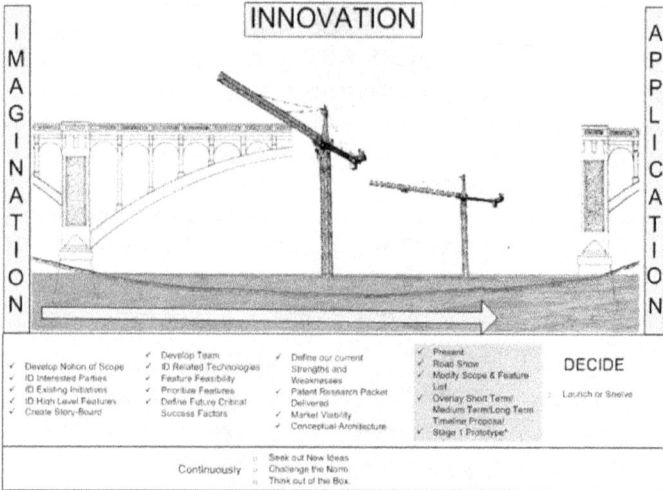

Figure 10. The Bridge Process

There is no way around this unless you are just going to "reinvent" someone else's solution. There is a huge gap between someone's "big idea" and creating a product. We have to bridge this gap. Fortunately, there is a method that works most of the time with our Innovative personalities. There are four phases of the Innovation Delivery Process.

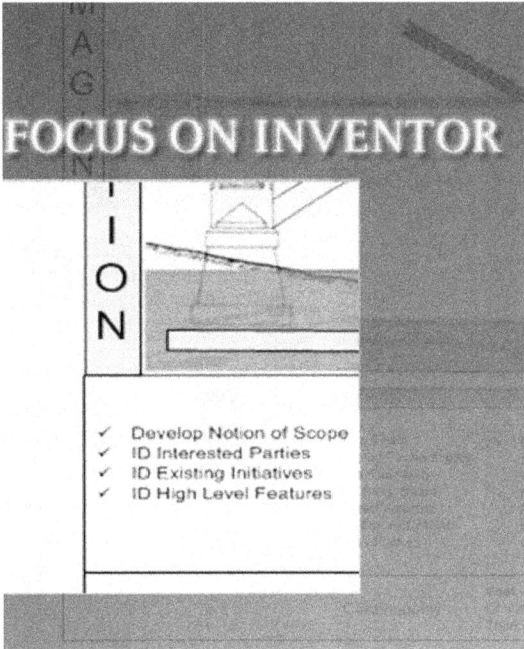

Figure 11. Focus on the Seer

Phase 1

In keeping with our personalities of innovation, the Pilot focuses on the Seer (Inventor.) Specifically, the Pilot will seek to understand the scope of the concept (the bigger the better at this point). Then, the Pilot seeks out the parties who would care. If you are inventing a new mobile app that will reduce crime, find a cop. If you are inventing the cure for the common cold, find a sick person and their doctor. Seers do not reach out to these resources.

There is too much risk that the interested parties might not like the idea. Now the Shapers really earn their money. They identify existing initiatives that either compete with this concept or complement it. Either way, you need to know this to pass the first "gate." Finally, Shapers begin to identify the features (not the functions). Some of these will start with the Seer, but most of the features will inevitably come from your Shapers and Builders. You might even consider dismissing the original "big idea" person from the conversation.

When you get done with Phase 1, you should have at a minimum:
- Scope (Pilot)
- Stakeholders (Pilot)
- Existing initiatives (Shapers)
- High level feature list (Shapers)

It is time for a "go/no-go" decision. Not all ideas are right for today or tomorrow. Some need to be put on the shelf for a month, six months, or a year. Let's be very careful here. Do NOT ask the following questions:
- Will this make money?
- Does this stand a chance in the market?
- How much money will this make?

Ask these questions instead:
- Do we have at least one Shaper, Builder, and Seer on board here?

- Do we have passion?
- Do we have a good idea of what the vision is?
- Is anyone else excited about this other than the Seer?

(Remember, the Pilot lives on the faith in the team).

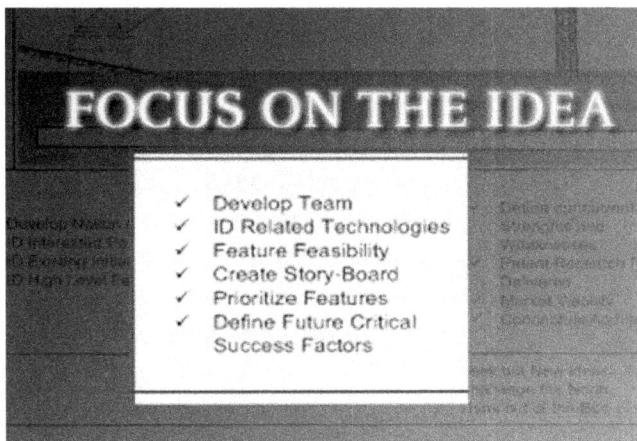

Figure 12. Focus on the Idea

Phase 2

This is the part that most everyone skips ahead to. Understandably, it's the most exciting part. That said, it's time to ditch Mr. or Mrs. Exciting (The Seer). Politely uninvite them. If you are the Seer, go away. The team needs your passion, but not for this phase. Don't worry—the team has your back or we wouldn't have made it past checkpoint 1. Here we focus on the idea itself.

You might be saying to yourself, "We went to all the trouble to get all the personalities together. Why did we just ditch the Seer?" Because when you exit Phase 2, you should have the following:

- The full stakeholders list
- Related technologies (competitive and noncompetitive)
- The feasibility of the feature set (columns labeled doable, cool, crazy, or use your own)
- A story or pitch board
- Prioritized features (this is why we booted the visionary—they think everything is great
- Future critical success factors identified

At the end of this phase, the go/no-go questions should look like this:

- Are there any other features you can think of?
- Do we like our prioritized features marked for "Present?"
- Do we have enough features? Aim for at least a dozen in three time-based categories: Present, Future, Out-There

Do NOT ask these questions:

- Is this product concept unique?
- Does this stand a chance in the market?

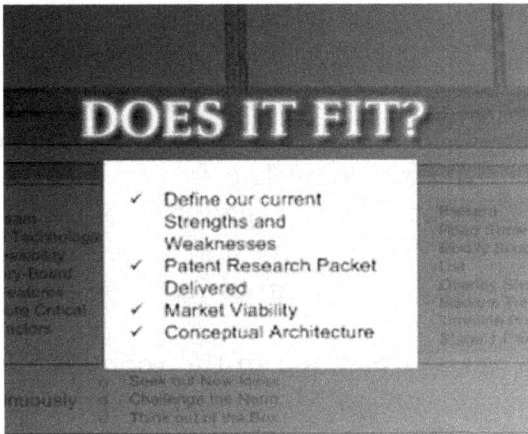

Figure 13. Does It Fit?

Phase 3

We now ask if this concept is right for to-day's or tomorrow's needs. Specifically, you should identify the following from Phase 3:

- Do we do this kind of thing well, or is it brand new for us?
- Is it patentable? If so, get started now (this is in the next chapter).
- What is the target market demographic? Do the best you can—this can be very hard to identify, and odds are you'll get this wrong to begin with.
- What would the market do if this landed today? What if it landed in six months? Remember that most innova-

tions have a shelf life of two to three years before they are met by competitive substitutions.

- Do we have a model drawn? This can be a "data flow model" or flow chart, but some kind of in-out drawing that depicts how the features of this concept will generate capital or efficiencies in it's target market and target demographic.

Get your Seer back in the room at this point for the "go/no-go" discussion. The right questions to ask are:

1. Are we the right people to bring this to market?

2. Can we protect this? Do we care?

3. What is our confidence in target market selection?

4. What is our Builder's confidence in the models we've drawn?

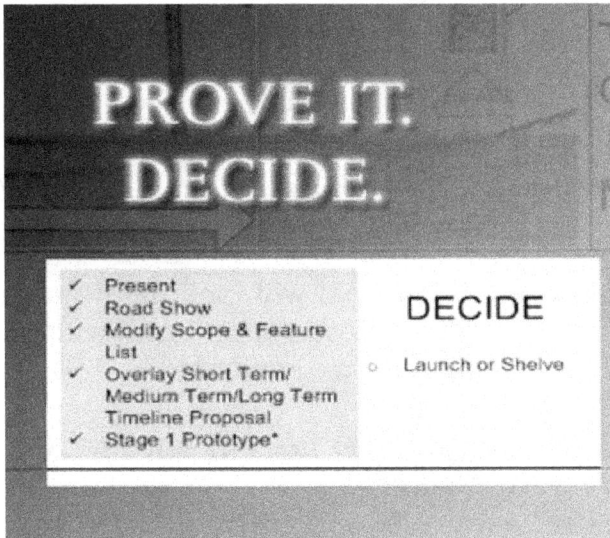

Figure 14. Prove It and Decide!

Phase 4

In this phase, we are ready for prime time. By now, we have stakeholders, storyboards, features, and functions, but most importantly, we have developed something that is priceless: We have created human momentum. One person busting into in investor's office and screaming that they have the answer that will make millions might get your attention for a minute or two. But 30 people entering the investor's office with all the materials from the first three phases is a homerun. Game over, cash the check, and move on.

In this phase your team will:

- Present the developed concept to a venture capitalist (VC), investor, or business leader.

- Based on feedback, we will modify the features and add new functions.

- Our proposal will include a timeline of short/medium/long term feature development and delivery.

- We will also present our first working prototype.

- Finally, we will decide to go to development or shelve the concept.

Here are the questions for consideration at the end of this phase:

- Do we have funding?

- Can we get to market fast enough?

- If the timing is not right, what is the tickler date (when we pull it back off the shelf for another shot)?

- Do we circle back around on our prototype and include additional features?

You have just crossed the bridge from an imaginary concept using innovation and applying a solution. For those traditional project managers out there who know what SDLC means, we have just completed a "pre-feasibility" phase.

Now armed with human momentum, models, working prototypes, and cash, it's time to build the final product or service and begin to reap the rewards. In the next section, we'll discuss some tools that you'll need to actually complete the vision. Traditional methods do not work any more. Time to the market has to be in days and weeks, not months—or by the time you implement, you'll be catching up to someone else. Since most of your final development will be born of the prototype, we will begin there.

GOATS ON YOUR LEMONADE STAND

11

PROTOTYPES

"A good example has twice the value of good advice."
Unknown Author

The P's of Prototyping

*P*assion: *If you don't have it, find it*

Not everyone is passionate about new ideas. But everyone has ideas. If you have an idea that you think will change the world, great. If not, find someone who does. Don't "interview" them. Be genuinely interested in what they have to say. Draw pictures, boxes, lines, whatever you have to do to ensure you "get it." Consider them your new business partner. Rarely can you be successful without your "visionary" in the room. You'll need them for funding, energy, and they're just a bunch of fun when you get the prototype built. There is usually crying, laughing, drinking, etc. You get the idea.

*P*rotection: *Hire an expensive IP attorney or....*

Consult with one and record the experience (call it an NDA if it makes the attorney more comfortable). In my opinion, the only thing better than having your own attorney is having one for a witness. Document the date of your "IP Consultation," and get them to sign off on the fact that you had the conversation. If you can afford your own attorney, great. If not, this little trick will at least get you over the hump. **Note: This little trick does not save you from doing a "previous art search." In the past, this meant flipping through dusty fat books in some state-owned building somewhere trying to see if someone else thought of it. These days, a great deal of this is on the Internet, but there is still no substitute for an attorney paying someone else to flip through dusty books. If you're on a budget, at least use your favorite search engine to make sure someone else hasn't stolen your idea 35 years ago.

**Note: Most Seers don't like to search for existing implementations of their idea. It is simply too devastating when they find out that the idea is not new. What they usually fail to think about is that it failed those ten times and is ripe for the picking now.

Productization: The cash flow maker.

The real magic begins: Here are the detailed steps for "productization."

- Draw three columns on a dry erase wall.

- Label them Present, Future, and Out There.
- Keep an area clear for issues, risks, and mitigations.

- Ask your Seer for what their idea is (or restate it if they are not there).

- Layout photos of your target demographic (I just cut photos from magazines).

- It is time for your Shapers to go to work. Ask them for a name for this product.

- List the features for the idea (all in the present column) on the Feature Board. Do not prioritize. Features should be marketable names like "car finder" or "potato pork chop."

- Now ask your Builders in the room to identify which ones might get out the door first. Remember that they think in the now so highlight those features up in the "Present" column.

- Align the remaining features you've discussed into the appropriate future columns.

- Now list the functions of each feature in the present column. For example, in your car, your radio is a feature of the car. It has multiple functions like CD player, FM/AM, etc.

- You now have the features and functions of the new product (Version 1). See Figure 15.

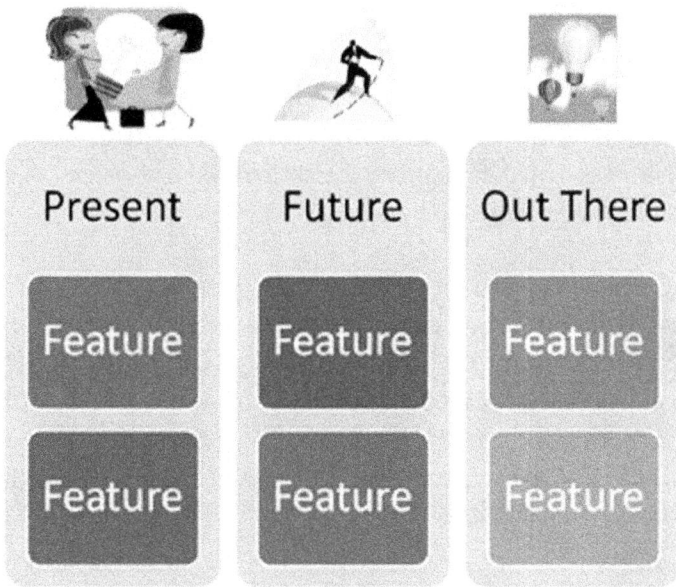

Figure 15. The Feature Board

Most people think they are done at this point and run off to marketing. The Seer is buying everyone drinks for listening to their dream. The Shaper is energized that he has something he can actually sink his teeth into. The Builder has already constructed a few of the present features in her head. Don't get too carried away. You've only just accomplished the plan for the prototype. It's time to build it.

Prototype: If it tastes like an apple, it's not an orange

It's a big, big deal for human beings to be able to touch, taste, and smell a concept. It makes it real and lasting.

Create a prototype for the concept. Make a cardboard box, wrap it in paper, and list the features on the back. Get your Builder involved, and get something that you can touch. This simple little effort will be what it takes to carry the new product idea to the VC or keep the team moving.

Piloting (not project managing)

Some of my favorite project managers are project managers. Unfortunately, they do get a bad rap. If you paid your neighbor's kids to build a snowman out of ice cubes in the tropics, you can't blame them when it melts. But we do. We have gone to all the work of defining our concept into a product, and now we ask a project manager to bring it home for us. However, since the project manager usually isn't there for the envisioning, they really don't stand much of a chance. On the other hand, the Pilot will have been there from the beginning. The Pilot's job is to build your project around the features of the concept itself. In other words, the work to be accomplished always rolls up to the feature.

INNOVATION CONCEPT

		Advertising	Engineering	Testing	
Feature 1	• Function 1	• 25k	• 5k	• 3k	
	• Function 2	• 18k	• 11k	• 4k	
Feature 2	• Function 1	• 72k	• 2k	• 5k	
	• Function 2	• 19k	• 9k	• 19k	
Feature 3	• Function 1	• 1k	• 11k	• 31k	
	• Function 2	• 9k	• 29k	• 49k	

Figure 16. The Feature Function Matrix

Getting something built is more than just having a project plan and executing on it. More often than not, good project managers see the project in a two dimensional way: Work to do on the left and time to accomplish on the right. In a different document, sometimes unrelated, we list stakeholders (the people you need to get the thing into production whom are billing you) like a contact book. In some other document, we list product capabilities. Here, we insist that you put all four of the elements into the same document. See Figure 16.

Everything including budget, milestones, parties, all roll up to a product feature. That way, we can tie all costs to the benefit (product feature). If the product feature isn't worth the cost (summed up across the stakeholders it takes to build it), don't build it. Or at least don't let your project manager build it...yet. At the end of the day - your new chart might look like Figure 17. Notice that we have eliminated functions that will not generate revenue, take market share, etc... We eliminate the feature or function for all stakeholders reducing costs before we even begin to talk about require- ments and specs. Now Version 1 of our innovation will include Feature 1 with Func- tion1, Feature 2 with Function 2, and only function 1 of Feature 3.

INNOVATION CONCEPT

		Advertising	Engineering	Testing
Feature 1	• Function 1	• 25k	• 5k	• 3k
	• Function 2	• 0	• 0	• 0
Feature 2	• Function 1	• 0	• 0	• 0
	• Function 2	• 19k	• 9k	• 19k
Feature 3	• Function 1	• 1k	• 11k	• 31k
	• Function 2	• 0	• 0	• 0

Figure 17. The Final Feature Matrix

Our product features and functions are listed down the left side. All requirements, recipes, drawings, etc. fall under these features. Now we list our stakeholders across the top so that any given feature has a number of people in- volved in getting the feature built (artists, mechanical engineers, coders, contractors).

Ask each stakeholder if the feature is bigger than a bread box (collect estimated hours to complete).When the cost from all the stakeholders for any given feature exceeds the value of the feature, don't write requirements for it, don't talk about it, and most certainly don't build the feature. There are some teams that build full books of requirements and blueprints (tens of thousands of dollars) on features they cannot afford to build. Dumb, huh? When they could have been using those dollars to build additional cheaper features that would generate income.

Bad stuff happens on innovation delivery projects. Unforeseen circumstances can occur that push the cost of the feature over the value. How do we track that? Run rates. For each feature we should have a summary of man-hours on the horizontal. For each stakeholder we should have a cost element per feature on the vertical. Folks, this is powerful: You get focused risk resilient project planning. This is value focused delivery dimensioning. Party on.

Putting into Practice

Seeing the future is easy; building it is hard; and implementing it is impossible. One simply cannot implement the future. Why? As soon as you implement it, it's no longer the future. It becomes something that we have to consider differently. Now we begin to think about sustainability, supportability, and training. Remember, we're building a bridge here. Yes, it's cool if we can move safely across this new bridge, but if it all crumbles behind us, there is no sustainable cash flow. Consider implementing mini-releases. Put your working prototype to work—even if it only has a couple features. Fear usually drives people to wait and put the whole product into production. If you wait, it's not innovation anymore.

By the way, I wasn't kidding when I mentioned parties above. Celebrate on the feature's release. Don't wait for your entire innovation to be completed. Celebrate the incremental successes—throw coals to that fire. I recommend loud music and balloons. "Hurray! We've finished the blah blah feature on the blah blah Product!!!" Party at the Seer's house—at this point, they'll usually buy all the required party materials.

PROTOTYPES

GOATS ON YOUR LEMONADE STAND

12

CLOSING THOUGHTS

I wish I could adequately describe the look on the face of the Seer when they see their vision become real. You should see the look of awe and gratitude on the faces of the Shapers and Builders who can look back on something they created together. When we tailor how we accomplish innovative delivery to the innovative personalities - the result is life changing. The closest thing I can think of to compare it to is the look on child's face when they sell that first cup of lemonade.

CLOSING THOUGHTS

Bibliography

Chapter quotes found at www.thinkexist.com.

Follow Jeff Deluca at
http://www.jeffdeluca.com

"MISSION"
From the album "Hold Your Fire"
Rush
Words by Neil Peart, Music by Geddy Lee and
Alex Lifeson

About the Author

Mike Duke has helped teams to apply for over two dozen patents and generate dozens of lemonade stands (prototypes.)

Mike owns at least one patent at the time of this writing and after speaking at several public forums, Mike was honored as one of **American Banker's top 25 innovators of the year - 2009.** Mike continues to speak to various groups about building lemonade stands and the personalities of innovation.

The Duke family now lives on a small farm east of Charlotte where they raise goats, chickens, 2 dogs, 1 rabbit, 1 angry fish, and 3 children.

One big, happy, innovative family.

You can follow Mike at
www.AreYouAGoat.com

www.ingramcontent.com/pod-product-compliance
Lightning Source LLC
Chambersburg PA
CBHW060635210326
41520CB00010B/1614

* 9 7 8 0 9 8 3 6 8 3 0 0 1 *